Basic Economics

BY

KARL BIEDENWEG, Ph.D.

ISBN 1–58037–090–X

Printing No. CD–1318

Mark Twain Media, Inc., Publishers
Distributed by Carson-Dellosa Publishing Company, Inc.

Table of Contents

FEDERAL BUILDING

Preface

The intent of this book is to introduce students to the basic principles of economics. Hopefully, by understanding the basic economic terms and concepts, students will apply this knowledge to their everyday lives. As the students watch a presidential address on television, hear the evening news, or read the newspaper, they will have a better understanding of why things change.

Each section of this book starts with an introduction and helpful insights for the student and teacher.

In every section, there are student activities in which students can apply what has been learned. The student activities may be copied for your students' use, or you may want to use the overhead so the entire class can participate at the same time.

An Internet activity is also included in each section. An Internet address has been provided for each activity. It is strongly suggested that you have your students do an additional search. This will give the students more practice using the Internet and make each student's assignment unique.

> "We call things we don't understand complex, but that means we haven't found a good way of thinking about them." —Tsutomu Shimomura

Section 1—What Is Economics?

Introduction

Economics is abstract compared to the concrete subjects that most students have studied to date. The hard and fast rules of mathematics, grammar, geography, and so on do not exist in the study of economics. Economics does provide many models and processes for guidance, in addition to empirical research which points us in certain directions. However, due to the human element involved in economic decision-making, this makes real-life economics somewhat ambiguous. It is important that you have a good working definition of economics and an understanding of the basic concepts. Furthermore, it is important that you can assimilate the definition and concepts into your own life. This will allow you to project these ideas onto other individuals and societies.

Defining Economics

Economics involves the research and evaluation of alternatives. We can apply the concepts of economics to our personal lives as well as to our society as a whole. Most scholars and practitioners view economics as the science of decision-making.

Economics is the study of the ways that individuals and societies allocate their limited resources in order to better satisfy their unlimited wants.

Dissection of the Definition

INDIVIDUAL decision-making is referred to as **microeconomics**.

SOCIETAL decision-making is referred to as **macroeconomics**.

To ALLOCATE means to divide among or to distribute in shares.

RESOURCES are the means to accomplish something.

WANTS are things that are needed or desired.

Economics describes the nature and behavior of an economy or of an economic system and investigates economic problems with the objective of offering solutions. The word *economy* is derived from the Greek words *oikos* (house) and *nemein* (to manage) and means, literally, "household management." We say that we practice economy when we are thrifty and sparing in the use of our resources. When we speak of an economy (like the American economy), we mean the orderly arrangement and management of production, exchange, and consumption in a household, business organization, community, or society.

Name____ Date_________________________

Student Activity 1.1

This exercise deals with identifying micro and macro issues. Indicate if each newspaper headline below deals with a micro or a macro issue.

__________ 1. Pepsi to Introduce a New Flavor

__________ 2. Russia Devalues Currency

__________ 3. Red Cross Needs Blood Desperately

__________ 4. Microsoft Still Tied-Up in Legal Battle

__________ 5. Federal Reserve Lowers Interest Rates

__________ 6. Congress to Tackle Social Security

__________ 7. Unemployment Reaches 20-Year Low

__________ 8. Catholic Church Recruits More Priests

__________ 9. Wal-Mart to Open 10 New Stores this Year

__________ 10. China Tries to Limit the Number of Births

__________ 11. YMCA Seeks Volunteers

__________ 12. U.S. Trade Deficit Widens

__________ 13. Library Extends Hours

__________ 14. CBS Has New Fall Line-Up

__________ 15. Michigan State Wins Four in a Row

Name ______________________________ Date ______________

Student Activity 1.2

1. Identify three decisions that you (micro) have made recently.

   a. ______________________________

   b. ______________________________

   c. ______________________________

2. Identify three decisions that our government (macro) has made recently.

   a. ______________________________

   b. ______________________________

   c. ______________________________

3. Identify three of your limited resources that you allocate daily.

   a. ______________________________

   b. ______________________________

   c. ______________________________

4. Identify three ways in which you come by these resources.

   a. ______________________________

   b. ______________________________

   c. ______________________________

5. Identify three material things of which you would like more (wants).

   a. ______________________________

   b. ______________________________

   c. ______________________________

Name____ Date________________________

Internet Activity #1

Describe the latest U.S. and international economic trends. Read the reports given at the Internet address below. Write a one-page paper, describing the current trends in your own words. Use the space below for your notes.

http://www.wellsfargo.com

Economic Reports and Commentary

Section 2—Individual and Family Scarcity and Limited Resources

Introduction

Scarcity is what economics is all about. The deeper our understanding of scarcity, the better we understand the essence of economics. Our desires and wants for goods and services are unlimited (individual, family, business, or society), while the resources to satisfy our desires and wants are limited.

Scarcity

Scarcity means we can never have all we want of every good and service.

Think about your answers to Question 5 in Student Activity 1.2. (Q: Identify three material things of which you would like more [wants].)

Now ask yourself why you do not get more of these things. The answers will revolve around the scarcity of resources. As humans, we have this insatiable appetite for more goods and services, but we lack the resources to satisfy our wants.

Limited Resources

List on the blackboard the limited resources the students in your class identified in Question 3 of Student Activity 1.2 (Q: Identify three of your limited resources that you allocate daily). Answers should include such things as time, money, energy, material things, capacity to learn, emotions, and the list can go on and on. These are all great examples of the limited resources that individuals and families have to decide how to allocate.

Decision-making on how individuals, families, businesses, and societies allocate limited (scarce) resources is what economics is all about.

"A mind, like a home, is furnished by its owner, so if one's life is cold and bare he can blame none but himself." —Louis L'Amour

Types of Societal Resources

Like individuals, societies cannot satisfy all their wants. All societies (in all countries) have limited resources. These resources are typically categorized into four groupings: land, labor, capital, and entrepreneurship.

LABOR is the human resource. Labor refers to the mental and physical efforts applied to the production of goods and services. Payments for labor services are called **wages**.

LAND is the environmental resource. Land includes all natural resources, land (including anything that grows on or below the land), water, air, and wildlife. Payments for the use of land are called **rents**.

CAPITAL is the physical improvement resource. Capital refers to all relatively permanent improvements made to land. Capital includes buildings, sidewalks, utilities that are installed, and all the machinery and equipment that is used to make the improvements. Another type of capital is financial capital, which includes money, stocks, bonds, and deeds to land. Payment for all capital is called **interest**.

ENTREPRENEURSHIP is the risk-taking resource. Entrepreneurs make things happen. They are the people who combine labor, land, and capital to start businesses. However, not every business is successful. As a matter of fact, more new businesses fail than survive. Payment for risk-taking or entrepreneurship is called **profit**.

Name________________________________ Date____________________

Student Activity 2.1

Calculating Simple Interest

Amount Borrowed x Interest Rate x Time = Interest

Note: Time is measured in years or fractions of years.

1. If you borrow $300 from the bank for a new mountain bike at a 6 percent interest rate payable in one year, how much interest would you pay?

      Interest paid
    + Original amount borrowed (principal)
    = Total amount paid for bike

___

2. If you received $400 for Christmas five years ago and put it in your piggy bank, with nothing added to it, how much would you have today?

___

3. If you had taken that $400 five years ago and placed it in a savings account receiving 5 percent interest, with nothing added to it, how much would you have today? (Hint: Add in interest for each year prior to calculating interest for the following year.)

   __________ the first year

   __________ the second year

   __________ the third year

   __________ the fourth year

   __________ the fifth year

4. If you borrowed $500 at 6 percent interest for five years, what would your monthly payment be (use simple interest method from Question 1 and divide by the total number of months)?

___

Name ______________________ Date ______________

Student Activity 2.2

On the basis of your observation, which factors of production are scarce at your school?

1. Labor:

   a. ______________________

   b. ______________________

   c. ______________________

2. Land:

   a. ______________________

   b. ______________________

   c. ______________________

3. Capital:

   a. ______________________

   b. ______________________

   c. ______________________

4. Entrepreneurship:

   a. ______________________

   b. ______________________

   c. ______________________

Name ____________________________ Date ________________

Internet Activity #2

What is the economic situation in the United States? How does the economic situation influence purchase decisions? Follow the path outlined below at the Internet address to find information about this topic. Write your answer in the space below.

http://www.odci.gov/cia

CIA Publications
The World Factbook
United States

Section 3—How Are Scarce Resources Allocated Among People?

Introduction

There are several different methods that can be used to allocate our scarce resources. There is no absolutely correct way of allocating scarce resources. A particular method might prove to be ideal in one situation but less satisfactory in other situations.

Methods of Allocation

MARKET SYSTEM is the method preferred in the United States. In our "free market system," what to produce, how much to produce, and the worth of goods and services, is decided by private buyers and sellers. Entrepreneurs seeing an opportunity for profits will produce and market a good or service. If the entrepreneur does a good job in anticipating the desires of the marketplace, then, through product sales, he or she will be rewarded with profits; on the other hand, if the entrepreneur does a poor job in anticipating the marketplace's desires, resulting in no or few sales, he or she will receive losses. Thus, it can be said that the market system (private buyers and sellers) allocates our scarce resources through the seller's willingness to produce goods and services and the buyer's willingness and ability to purchase goods and services.

BRUTE FORCE is another way of deciding who gets what. We see this method used in the animal kingdom. The biggest, strongest, and/or fastest animals get what they want. This method is usually very wasteful. The weaker individuals do not get enough scarce resources to survive properly or do not receive enough resources to become more productive. The stronger thugs tend to become fat and lazy, wasting scarce resources or not using them efficiently.

QUEUING (lining up) is another method for deciding who gets what. This method is based on the principle of first come/first served. This might be the preferred method of selling concert tickets, but this method has some inherent flaws. First, if this were the primary method for allocating all our scarce resources, too much of our time would be wasted standing in lines, and not enough time would be devoted to production. Also, when scarce resources get really limited, the purchase price rises, sometimes causing a black or underground market to develop. We have seen this happen at sporting events, when scalpers resell tickets for many times their original value.

RANDOM SELECTION is when everyone has an equal chance. Allocation through random selection can be accomplished by drawing names out of a hat, by drawing straws, or by using more sophisticated methods generated by computers and random number tables. On the surface, this sounds like a good method for allocating scarce resources, and in some situations it is. However, it is not a good method in all situations. For example, if jobs were allocated by random selection, some of us might get the perfect job, one that we may never have gotten using any other method. But many people will receive jobs they are unqualified for or simply do not like. They will be like round pegs in square holes. Overall production will suffer.

TRADITION may be used to allocate scarce resources. What was done in the past is what will be done in the future. Tradition assumes that things do not change and that if it worked well in the past, it will work as well in the future. Some of you might have studied the caste systems of India and feudal European monarchies; these were based on tradition. If your father was a musician, then you were to become a musician, regardless of whether you had willingness and talent. Obviously many resources and talents are wasted when tradition is used as a basis for allocation.

EQUAL SHARES is when each individual receives the same amount. Occasionally this may be the best method for allocating scarce resources. For example, if you and your friend only have 10 minutes left to play a video game, each of you could play for five minutes, which would be fair. On a larger scale, however, this method might not be as fair, and many times it is very wasteful. For example, if everyone received an equal amount of food, then a person weighing 100 pounds may have too much food and some will be wasted, and a person weighing 200 pounds may not have enough food and will get sick. The problem is compounded by some people disliking some foods and others being allergic to some foods.

NEED as a basis for resource allocation refers to those who appear to be the neediest going to the head of the line. It is extremely difficult to determine when another individual falls into this "needy" category. It is even more difficult to determine when this individual is no longer in need. Many times being needy is a value judgment based on one's own background. Many times need is based on hardships, but there are many tragic examples of people exaggerating their hardships or creating self-induced hardships to qualify as "needy."

PLANNED SYSTEMS exist in mostly socialist countries. Government planners decide what and how much is to be produced and distributed by whom, when, and to whom. Producers generally have little choice about what goods and services they will produce. Their main task is to meet their assigned production quotas. Prices are set by government planners and do not change according to supply and demand. In some situations, government planning works fairly well, as long as the economy is simple and the variety of goods and services desired is small. Furthermore, planned systems might even be necessary under certain conditions, during wartime, for example.

The best method for allocating scarce resources is to look at the situation and participants first and then to determine the tool for allocation.

Name _______________________________ Date ___________________

Student Activity 3.1

Use a real-life example to describe the following allocation methods. Hint: Use family, friends, teams, church, and/or clubs for examples.

1. Brute Force ____

2. Queuing ____

3. Random Selection ____

4. Tradition ____

5. Equal Shares ____

6. Need ____

Name_______________________________ Date_______________

Student Activity 3.2

Write a short paper comparing and contrasting "market systems" and "planned economic systems." Use the space provided below for your outline.

Name ______________________________ Date ____________________

Internet Activity #3

Summarize the economics of the Internet. Describe the history and current state of the Internet, along with the economic and regulation problems. Follow the path outlined below at the Internet address to find information about this topic. Use the space below for your notes.

http://www.sims.berkeley.edu/resources

Infocon
Background and References
FAQs
Economic FAQs About the Internet

Section 4—Institutions That Affect Economic Behavior

Introduction

The principles of economics do not take place in a vacuum. In this section, we will discuss the major institutions that shape and are shaped by economic behavior. The three major institutions are: households, businesses, and, in Section 5, the government's impact on economics.

Households

Households provide some of the resources needed by businesses. Households consume many of the goods produced by businesses, and the members of households are the ultimate owners of wealth.

Households provide labor, land, capital, and entrepreneurial skills to businesses.

Households consume automobiles, food, clothing, and a host of other products produced by businesses.

Businesses and all the assets they use are owned ultimately by individual households. Thus, businesses ultimately do not receive profits; they are only the middlemen who channel profits to the owners of the businesses, who are the individuals of households.

Types of Business Ownership

There are three legal forms of businesses that can be established in the United States. Businesses may be operated as **sole proprietorships**, **partnerships**, or **corporations.**

A **SOLE PROPRIETORSHIP** is the easiest type of business to establish. Registering with the state and getting a federal tax number is about all it takes in most cases. As the proprietor, you are the owner and boss. The amount of profit you make depends on your skill, hard work, and luck.

The basic advantages associated with a sole proprietorship are (1) it is easy to start up, (2) it is simple to manage, and (3) it is relatively free from government regulation.

But on the other side of the coin there are some distinct disadvantages, which are (1) getting financed is limited by the wealth and credit standing of the proprietor, (2) the business dies when the proprietor dies or quits, and (3) unlimited liability of the proprietor (both business and personal assets may be lost if the business fails or becomes a losing party in a lawsuit).

In a **PARTNERSHIP**, two or more individuals combine to form a business so they can overcome some of the financial and managerial disadvantages of sole proprietorships.

The advantages associated with partnerships would include (1) it is easy to start up, (2) it is relatively simple to manage, and (3) it is subject to relatively few government regulations.

Disadvantages of a partnership include (1) unlimited liability of partners (if your partner makes a mistake or is dishonest, your personal assets may be in jeopardy), (2) division of ownership often leads to disagreements in operations and management of the business, and (3) the death or withdrawal of one partner dissolves the partnership, although a new organization may be formed.

CORPORATIONS are organizations sanctioned by state laws and are considered "legal entities" separate and distinct from the owners. To start a corporation, you are required to submit a "charter" to the state government outlining the type of business intended. The charter should also specify how the corporation will be financed and governed.

The advantages of a corporation over other types of businesses would include (1) it is easier to finance because a corporation can sell stocks and bonds, (2) limited owner liability (the stockholders can only lose their investment), (3) unlimited life (the death of a stockholder does not mean the end of a corporation), and (4) highly specialized management.

The disadvantages of a corporation are (1) it is more difficult to start up, and (2) it is subject to extensive government regulation and taxation.

"Whenever you see a successful business, someone once made a courageous decision." —Peter Drucker

Name ______________________________ Date ______________

Student Activity 4.1

Each type of business (sole proprietorship, partnership, and corporation) uses different methods for distributing the profits to the owners.

Sole proprietorship—All profits are distributed to the sole owner, as he or she has taken all the risks.

Partnership—Typically profits are distributed based on the percentage of capital invested. If one partner invested more than the others, then this partner has more at risk.

Corporation—Profits are distributed to the stockholders. Preferred stock is paid first, then any remaining profits are distributed to the common stock.

1. If you were a sole proprietor and had annual profits of $100,000, how would the profits be distributed?

____

____

2. If you were partners with Alice and Mark (you contributed 50 percent of the capital, Alice contributed 30 percent, and Mark contributed 20 percent), how would the annual profits of $100,000 be distributed?

   You ______________

   Alice ______________

   Mark ______________

3. Using the numbers from Problem 2, how would an annual **loss** of $80,000 be distributed?

   You ______________

   Alice ______________

   Mark ______________

Name____________________________ Date________________

Student Activity 4.1 (continued)

4. A corporation has 1,000 shares of preferred stock and 4,000 shares of common stock. The preferred stock has a prior claim to an annual $8 dividend. If the annual profits to be distributed for the first three years were $20,000, $35,000, and $60,000 respectively, how much would be distributed to preferred stock and common stock? Also, calculate the dividends per share. Use the blank space below for your calculations.

	First Year	**Second Year**	**Third Year**
Preferred Stock	________	________	________
Common Stock	________	________	________
Dividend Per Share			
Preferred	________	________	________
Common	________	________	________

"To acquire knowledge, one must study; but to acquire wisdom, one must observe." —Marilyn vos Savant

Name________________________________ Date____________________

Student Activity 4.2

There are other alternate methods of allocating profits and losses in a partnership. Allocation could be based on equal division, the amount of original investment of each partner, or the amount of time devoted to the business by each partner.

1. Mary and Carla have decided to form a partnership. They have agreed that Mary is to invest $20,000 and Carla is to invest $30,000. Mary is to devote full time to the business and Carla is to devote one-half time. Determine the division of income under each of the following assumptions. Use the blank space below for your calculations.

Plan	**$30,000 Income**		**$15,000 Income**	
	Mary	**Carla**	**Mary**	**Carla**
Equal Division	________	________	________	________
Original Investment	________	________	________	________
Time Devoted	________	________	________	________

"There is the risk you cannot afford to take, and there is the risk you cannot afford not to take." —Peter Drucker

Name ______________________________ Date ______________________

Internet Activity #4

Select and analyze three monthly economic indicators that would be important to a restaurant chain. Follow the path outlined below at the Internet address to find information about this topic. Prepare a one-page report on your findings. Use the space below for your notes.

http://www.census.gov/ftp/pub/indicator

Parent Discovery
Current Economic Indicators

Section 5—Government's Effect on Economic Behavior

Introduction

Did you ever wonder why the founders of the United States formed our government and what its major economic responsibilities are? The answer is really quite simple. The government was formed to address the weaknesses of our market-directed economic system. In our market-directed system, individuals and businesses experience a high degree of choice. Humans, especially Americans, tend to be very self-centered. Consequently, many make sure they are taken care of first before helping the less fortunate. Further, there are some things that government can collectively take care of more efficiently than people or businesses can individually. Let's examine three of the major economic responsibilities of our government.

Setting the Rules of the Game

Through its legislative authority, the government sets rules establishing the legal relationships between parties. Further, the government sets monetary standards, insures bank deposits, and pursues a variety of other activities to protect public confidence. Perhaps the government's greatest economic responsibility is to maintain competition. The government has established many anti-trust (anti-monopoly) laws that govern competition. Where competition is impractical, government regulation is used to protect society from the abuses of monopoly power.

Income Redistribution

Nobody wants to see others suffer, go without shelter, or go without food. Some people freely give time and money to help the less fortunate. But, in most cases, it is not enough to service all those in need. Thus, through government programs such as Aid to Families with Dependent Children, food stamps, social security, and disaster relief, just to name a few, the taxed income of the population is redistributed to those in need.

Stabilization of Income, Prices, and Employment

There are natural "business cycles" that cause fluctuations in employment, income, and prices. Many times business cycles will cause inflation, dislocate workers, and cause prices to rise. The government tries to stabilize these factors by setting interest rates, controlling monetary growth, setting tax rates and depreciation rates, and through government spending.

> "There is no art which one government sooner learns of another than that of draining money from the pockets of the people." —Adam Smith

Name ______________________________ Date ____________________

Student Activity 5.1

What else does our government do with tax money?

Through your own experience, by asking your parents, by watching the national news, or by reading a newspaper, identify at least 10 things our government spends our tax money on.

1. ____

2. ____

3. ____

4. ____

5. ____

6. ____

7. ____

8. ____

9. ____

10. ____

Name ______________________________ Date ______________

Student Activity 5.2

What benefits do you and your family receive from government spending? Identify 10 government expenditures and explain in what way you and/or your family benefit.

1. ______________________________

2. ______________________________

3. ______________________________

4. ______________________________

5. ______________________________

6. ______________________________

7. ______________________________

8. ______________________________

9. ______________________________

10. ______________________________

"Income-tax time is when you test your powers of deduction." —Shelly Friedman

Name ______________________________ Date ____________________

Internet Activity #5

Your future personal and family income hinges on what career you choose. Check out the Internet address below, choose a career field, and write a one-page report on future job opportunities, income, and other related information. Follow the path outlined below at the Internet address to find information about this topic. Use the space below for your notes.

http://stats.bls.gov

Publications
Occupational Outlook Handbook
Occupational Cluster
Outlook for Specific Occupations

Section 6—Supply and Demand

Introduction

So far we have discussed some of the fundamental concepts of economics. In Section 1, we covered the definition of economics, and in Sections 2 and 3, we addressed limited resources and scarcity. In Sections 4 and 5, we discussed the institutional forces that affect economic behavior, that is, the households, firms, and governmental organizations that interact to produce and distribute goods and services. Now we are ready to look at supply and demand, which are the major factors that explain the operation of our market economy.

The concepts of supply and demand, along with elastic and inelastic demand, are where most students get confused and frustrated about economics. It is very important that these topics are covered slowly and thoroughly, because these concepts are the cornerstone of economics.

Before we get into the dreaded supply and demand graphs, let's do some wordsmithing.

LAW OF DIMINISHING DEMAND states that as the demand price goes up, so will the supply of a given good or service. Further, as the demand price goes down, so will the supply.

DEMAND CURVE shows the amount of goods and services that will be purchased at various prices.

SUBSTITUTES are alternative goods or services that offer a choice to buyers. The greater the number of substitutes, the greater the degree of elasticity.

ELASTIC DEMAND means that as the price fluctuates, so does demand. As prices increase the demand goes down, and as prices drop demand goes up.

INELASTIC DEMAND means that as the price fluctuates up or down (within a relevant range), demand remains constant.

SUPPLY CURVE shows the amount of goods or services that will be made available and sold at various prices.

MARKET EQUILIBRIUM POINT is the point at which the quantity and the price sellers are willing to offer is equal to the quantity and price that buyers are willing to accept.

"Forecasting is like trying to drive a car blindfolded and following directions given by a person who is looking out of the back window." —Anonymous

Law of Diminishing Demand

Most families budget a certain amount of money to spend on groceries per week. If the consumer is mainly interested in buying a certain amount of food stuff and the price of hamburger drops, it seems reasonable to expect that he or she will switch some of his or her food money to hamburger and away from some other foods. But, on the other hand, if the price of hamburger rises, you would expect the consumer to buy less hamburger and more of other foods. This example represents the **law of diminishing demand**.

Demand Curve

If we were to plot on a graph how much hamburger consumers would purchase at different prices, we would have a **demand curve** similar to the one shown below.

Demand Curve for Hamburger

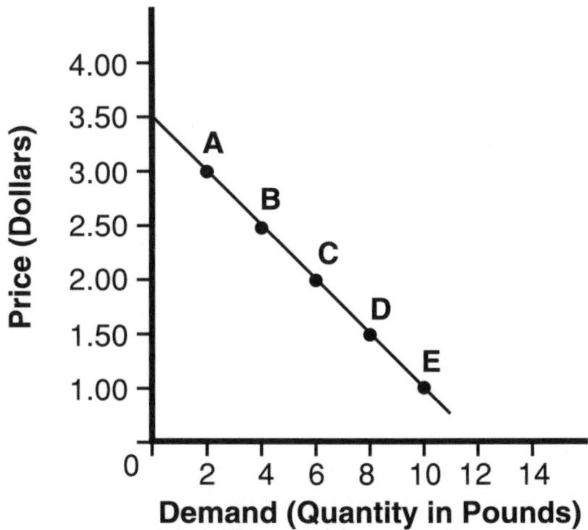

With all these prices and quantities to choose from, how does one know what the best price is? If you are the consumer (buyer), the lower the price, the better. If you are the seller, then you would want to set the price that would yield the greatest total revenue. The easiest way of comparing different price levels is to make a **demand schedule** like the one below.

Point	Price per lb.	Quantity in lbs.	Total Revenue	
A	$3.00	2	$6	
B	$2.50	4	$10	
C	$2.00	6	$12	← $12.25
D	$1.50	8	$12	
E	$1.00	10	$10	

Based on this demand schedule, the price that would yield the highest total revenue for the seller would be between $1.50 and $2.00; they both would yield $12.00. At the price of $1.75, the seller should sell 7 pounds, which would be the optimum price ($1.75 x 7 = $12.25).

Elastic Demand

All products do not have the same demand curve. Because of the great number of **substitutes** for hamburger, demand will fluctuate (up or down) depending on its selling price. This fluctuating demand is called **elastic demand**. Looking at the demand schedule mathematically, we see that price and total revenue move in opposite directions.

Inelastic Demand

If a certain product, such as gasoline, does not have many good substitutes, the demand will remain the same as long as there is not quick, radical change in price. Let's look at a demand curve for gasoline.

Demand Curve for Gasoline

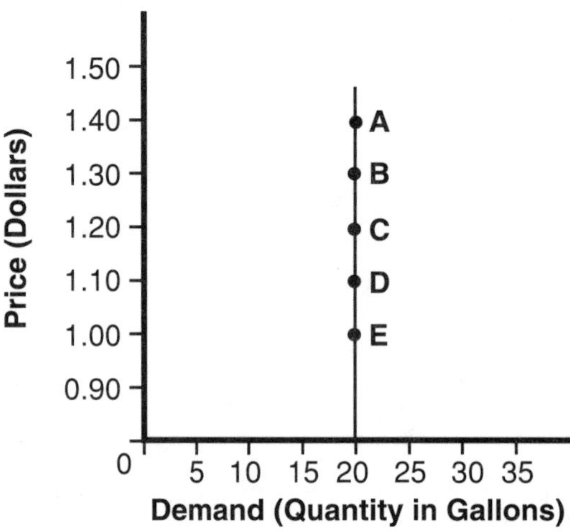

As we can see from the demand curve, relatively small changes in price (up or down) will not change people's driving habits, so the demand will stay the same. When demand stays relatively constant with small percentage changes in price, this is referred to as **inelastic demand**.

Let's construct a demand schedule for gasoline.

Point	Price per Gallon	Quantity in Gallons	Total Revenue
A	$1.40	20	$28.00
B	$1.30	20	$26.00
C	$1.20	20	$24.00
D	$1.10	20	$22.00
E	$1.00	20	$20.00

As you might have noticed, as price goes down, so does total revenue. On the other hand, as price goes up, so does total revenue. When price and total revenue move in the same direction, this indicates inelastic demand. The optimum price for the seller would be at the highest level where price does not affect demand.

Supply Curve

So far, things should make sense. This is because of our simple example in which we have one seller and one buyer. We still need to factor in suppliers. In remembering the law of diminishing demand, as the demand price rises, so does the supply quantity, and as supply increases, prices tend to decrease.

With this in mind, the market price for gasoline will be driven downward by increased supply if the price was set at the top of the demand curve. This is because at very high prices more firms are willing to supply the market.

How much suppliers are willing to release into the market depends on the price they can receive. Typically, the higher the price, the more suppliers will release to the market.

We can see how this works by looking at a **supply curve**.

Supply Curve for Gasoline

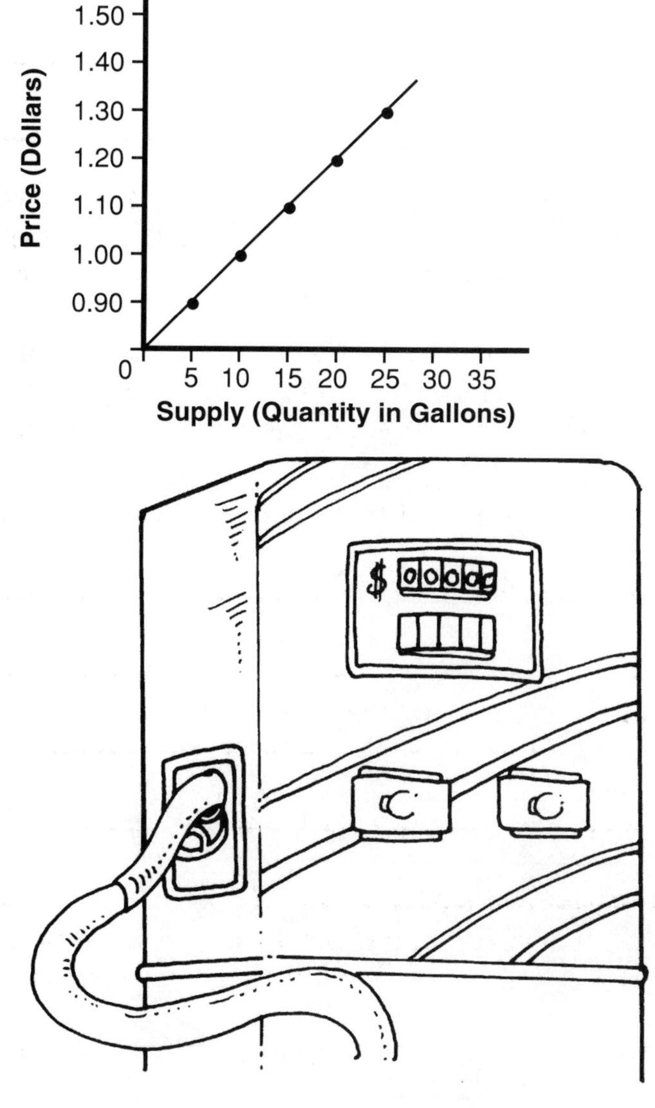

Market Equilibrium Point

Suppliers want to maximize their total revenue, just as sellers do. So when the quantity and price that sellers are willing to offer are equal to the quantity and price that buyers are willing to accept, then they have reached the **market equilibrium point**. The following graph shows the equilibrium point for gasoline.

Demand and Supply Curve for Gasoline

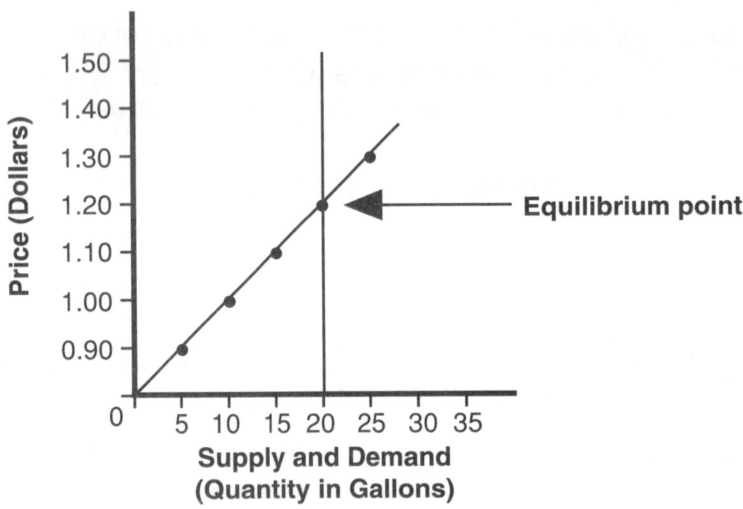

When we combine the gasoline demand curve and supply curve, we can see that the equilibrium point is $1.20.

SUPPLY & DEMAND

Name_______________________________________ Date_______________________

Student Activity 6.1

Equilibrium Point

Use the demand curve already given for hamburger.

1. Draw a supply curve and a supply schedule.

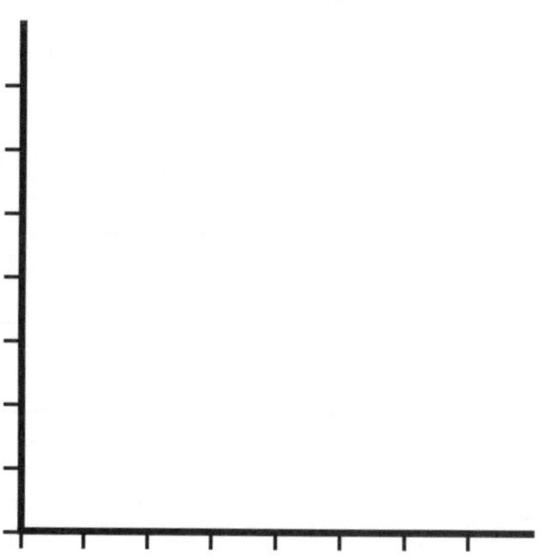

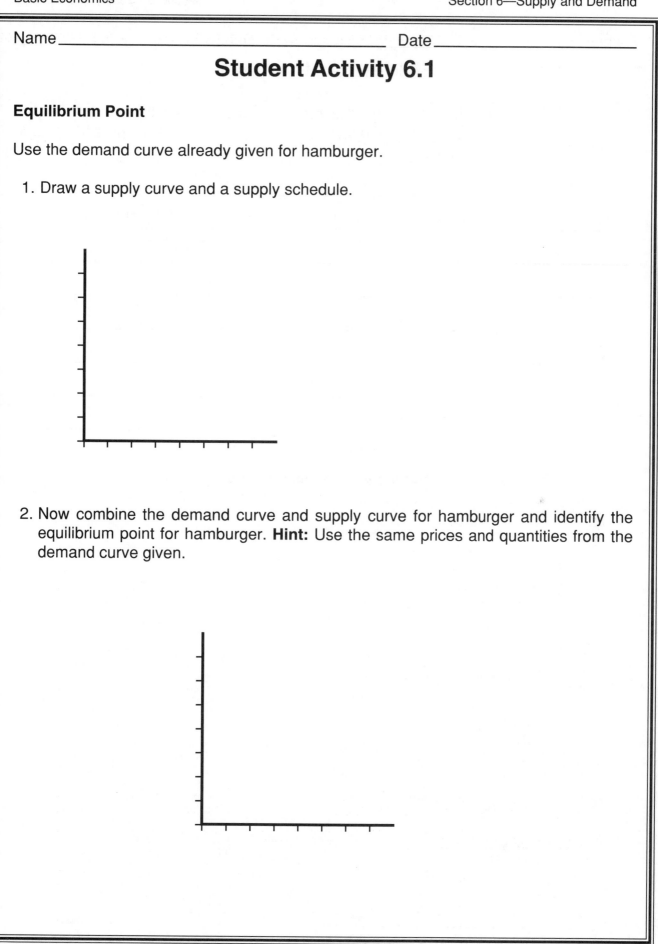

2. Now combine the demand curve and supply curve for hamburger and identify the equilibrium point for hamburger. **Hint:** Use the same prices and quantities from the demand curve given.

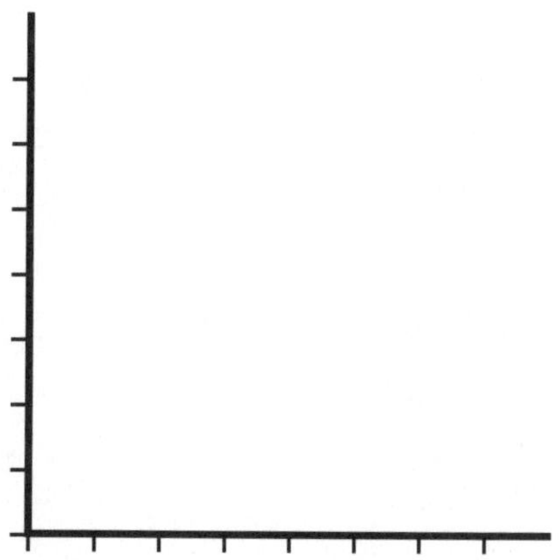

Name ____________________ Date ____________

Student Activity 6.2

From the newspaper came this story: "Record Number of Baseball Fans Paid Higher Prices." Explain how this situation could have occurred, and then use supply and demand curves to illustrate your answer.

____

____

____

____

____

____

____

____

Supply and Demand Curves

Name ______________________________ Date ______________

Internet Activity #6

Competition and comparable substitution are what help determine the market price. Assume you just bought a hotel in San Francisco and you want to evaluate your guest room rates. Currently, king rooms at your hotel are priced at $225 per night. Identify other San Francisco hotels that offer comparably-priced rooms. What are their rates for king rooms? What hotels offer the best value (price and features)? Follow the path outlined below at the Internet address to find information about this topic. Write your answers in the space below.

http://www.hotelres.com

Hotel Search
Enter Next Monday's Date
Make Selections for Comparison

Section 7—How Unemployment Influences Our Economics

Introduction

The President's Council of Economic Advisors uses the following process to measure unemployment.

Persons are classified as unemployed if they were not employed during the survey week, but were available for work and had made a specific effort to find a job at some time within the preceding four weeks, or if they were waiting either to report to a new job within 30 days or be recalled to a job from which they were laid off.

This weekly survey and classification process determines the unemployment rate. There is a very large sample, which ensures the data collected by the Department of Labor are reasonably reliable. But most researchers know that these statistics are not completely accurate. This is due to two distinct groups, **discouraged workers** and **dishonest non-workers**, which fluctuate in size.

DISCOURAGED WORKERS are individuals who would love to go back to work, but due to the length of time being unemployed, low self-esteem, many job application rejections, or just bad luck, they have given up on looking for a new job. These individuals are beyond the four-week cutoff for counting them as unemployed, thus the real rate of unemployment is underestimated.

DISHONEST NON-WORKERS are individuals who say they are looking for employment, thus being eligible for unemployment compensation, although they have no real intention of taking a new job. Therefore, because of this group, the real rate of unemployment is overestimated.

Ask yourself why and when (under what circumstances) the sizes of these groups might be larger or smaller.

> "Work is a mysterious thing; many of us claim to hate it, but it takes a grip on us that is so fierce that it captures emotions and loyalties we never knew were there." —Bob Greene

Basic Classifications of Unemployment

1. **FRICTIONAL UNEMPLOYMENT** is when unemployment happens naturally. That is, there are some people who quit their jobs because they do not like them, and some people seek to re-enter the job market (like mothers after leaving a job to have children).

2. **STRUCTURAL UNEMPLOYMENT** occurs when the skills of the potential employee no longer match the needs of potential employers. Technological changes may have made an employee's skills and talents obsolete. For example, someone who specialized in automotive carburetor repair is in less demand today because most cars are fuel-injected.

3. **SEASONAL UNEMPLOYMENT** happens because some products/businesses are in demand during only part of the year. The construction business in the northern states and agriculture harvesting in many states are good examples. When business is not being conducted, the demand for employees drops considerably.

4. **CYCLICAL UNEMPLOYMENT** is a result of the business cycles referred to earlier. There is a seemingly natural cycle of good economic times and poor times. During these poor times of recession or depression, businesses decrease their outputs, which requires fewer employees, thus causing an increase in unemployment.

5. **INDUCED UNEMPLOYMENT** is caused by governmental policy. A prime example is the national minimum wage law. The minimum wage law prevents businesses from hiring workers who would otherwise work for less pay than the government law requires.

> "Careers, like rockets, don't always take off on schedule. The key is to keep working on the engines." —Gary Sinise

Name ______________________ Date ______________

Student Activity 7.1

Negative and Positive Effects of Unemployment

1. From a family perspective, what would be a negative effect of unemployment?

____

____

____

2. How does an increase in unemployment negatively affect our government?

____

____

____

3. If an employee gets laid off, why might this present an opportunity to him/her?

____

____

____

____

4. When a business finds it necessary to lay off some employees (due to slowing sales), what positive effects might this have for the business?

____

____

____

____

5. Mr. Smith was disabled in a car accident in 1995 and has not been able to work since. Is Mr. Smith included in the unemployment statistics? Why or why not?

____

____

____

Name ______________________________ Date ______________________

Student Activity 7.2

For the following situations, identify the type of unemployment each represents.

1. Because of the decline in the U.S. birth rate, baby clothes manufacturers are laying off workers.

____

____

2. Bill decided to relocate to Texas. He quit his present job and found a new job in Texas three weeks later.

____

____

3. As interest rates continue to rise, the sale of new homes decreases. This has caused an increase of unemployed construction workers.

____

____

4. As the fall harvest ends, agriculture unemployment increases.

____

____

5. Janet worked in the drive-up window of a bank. The bank has installed an automated teller machine and has closed the drive-up window. Janet's job no longer exists, so she has to start looking for another job.

____

____

6. The state of Missouri has enacted a law stating that no one under the age of 21 can work in an establishment that sells liquor. Mark, an 18-year-old, was working as a waiter in a restaurant that sells alcoholic beverages. He can no longer work at the restaurant.

____

____

Name ______________________________ Date ______________

Internet Activity #7

Describe the importance of price in the purchasing decision for personal computers. Read several articles and write a one-page report on the topic. Follow the path outlined below at the Internet address to find information about this topic. Use the space below for your notes.

http://www.dejanews.com

Channels—Computers & Science
Quick Search (try several word combinations)

Section 8—Competitive Situations

Introduction

The competitive situation refers to the number and type of competitors that a particular firm must deal with, along with some predictions on how the competitors are likely to behave.

There are four basic competitive situations. Let's discuss some basic characteristics which differentiate the situations. Then the class (as a group or individually) can fill out the blank table in Student Activity 8.1.

Four Basic Competitive Situations

There are four basic competitive situations: pure competition, monopolistic competition, oligopoly competition, and monopoly. Let's identify a few basic characteristics that help us determine the competitive situation.

PURE COMPETITION

Pure competition is a market situation that typically has the following characteristics:

1. There are many buyers and sellers.
2. The products are very similar; many times the products are identical.
3. It is easy for buyers and sellers to get into and out of the market.

A good example of a pure competitive market situation would be farmers who raise carrots.

1. There are many farmers and consumers of carrots.
2. Unless it is a special variety of carrot, the consumers do not know or care if they are buying Farmer Brown's or Farmer Smith's carrots at the grocery store.
3. It is "relatively" easy to become a carrot farmer.

NOTE: Because there are so many producers of similar products, no one producer has control over price. If Farmer Brown raised his price of carrots, no one would buy them because there are thousands of other producers willing to sell their carrots at a lower price. If Farmer Brown lowered his price, he would easily sell his carrots, but his total revenue would probably remain the same or he might even lose money by selling at a lower price. In pure competitive market situations, individual producers have no control over price, so it is said that they sell at "the going market rate."

MONOPOLISTIC COMPETITION

Monopolistic competition is a market situation that typically has the following characteristics:

1. Sellers who offer different products (sometimes the products are not really very different, but buyers believe they are).
2. Sellers believe they have competition (the number can vary greatly).

A good example of monopolistic competition would be laundry soap manufacturers.

1. Most consumers believe laundry soaps are different. If you asked your mother or grandmother which laundry soap was the best, almost all of them would have a very definite answer. However, *Consumer's Report* did a study on the leading laundry soaps and came to the conclusion that there were not any significant differences among them. To further make consumers believe the laundry soaps are different, manufacturers add bleach to some and fabric softeners to others.
2. There are several manufacturers of laundry soap.

NOTE: Because laundry soap manufacturers have done a good job of convincing consumers that some laundry soaps work better than others, those manufacturers can charge more for their soaps. Thus, it is said that in monopolistic competition, firms have some control over price because the consumers see a difference in product offerings. Further, the demand curve tends to be elastic, as described earlier.

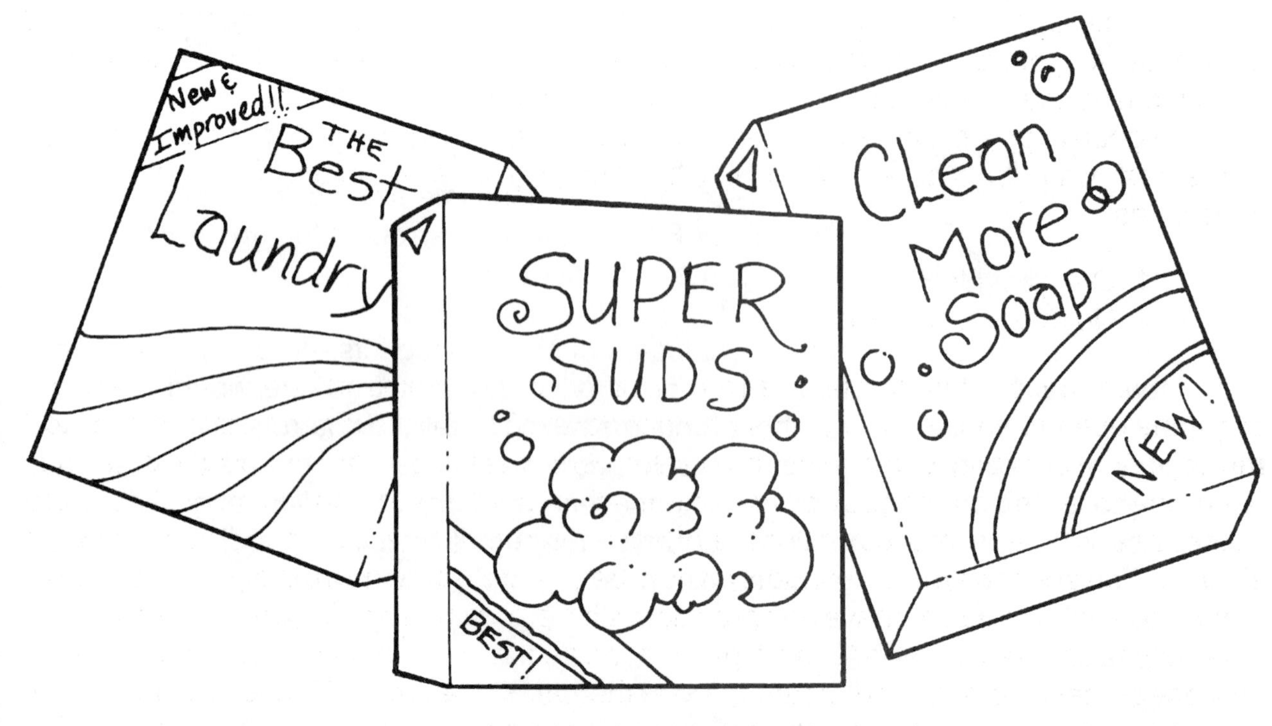

OLIGOPOLY COMPETITION

Oligopoly competition is a market situation that typically has the following characteristics:

1. The products offered by the sellers are very similar.
2. There are only a few sellers or just a few big competitors who dominate the market.

A good example of oligopoly competition would be long distance telephone companies.

1. The long distance telephone service is basically the same, no matter which long distance telephone company you use.
2. AT&T, MCI, and Sprint dominate the long distance telephone industry.

NOTE: When it comes to pricing, the different oligopoly competitors have little control over price. If one long distance company charges too high of a price, then individuals will change to a different long distance company. Further, if one company lowers their prices and starts to take away market share from the others, then typically the other firms will lower their prices also. This is when a "price war" starts, and all the sellers lose. Consequently, oligopoly competitors watch the market carefully and only make slight price adjustments. Further, the demand curve tends to be inelastic, as described earlier.

MONOPOLY

A **monopoly** market situation is truly different than the other three market situations. In order to have a true monopoly, you must be the only provider and there must be NO good substitutes for your product. In the United States, one would be very hard pressed to think of an industry that consisted of only one producer and no substitutes.

A good hypothetical example of a monopoly would be a person or firm that controlled all the fresh water on a desert island. In this example, you have one provider and NO good substitutes.

1. One provider.
2. No good substitutes.

Even though it is difficult to come up with real examples of true monopolies, our economy does have two other types of monopolies. The first is a **government-granted monopoly**. Most utility companies are government-granted monopolies. Many of us only have one local telephone provider or one electric company to choose from. There are substitutes for these products, but the substitutes are not very practical given today's lifestyle. The second type of monopoly would be a **geographic monopoly**. A geographic monopoly is when you only have one provider within a certain geographic area. People from small towns can easily relate to this type of market situation. In many small towns, there is only one grocery store, one dry cleaner, or one theater. These firms TEND to have monopoly characteristics because they are the only provider and because there do not seem to be any good substitutes.

Name ________________________________ Date ____________________

Student Activity 8.1

1. Fill out the following chart based on what has been discussed so far.

	Pure Competition	Monopolistic Competition	Oligopoly Competition	Monopoly
A. Example not already used				
B. Number of competitors				
C. Similarity of firm's offering				
D. Market strength of any one firm				
E. Firm's control over price				
F. Ease of entry for competitors resource-wise				
G. Elasticity of demand				

Name________________________________ Date____________________

Student Activity 8.2

It is not as easy as it might seem to correctly identify a firm's competitive situation. When trying to correctly identify the competitive situation, it is important that you look at many characteristics. Looking at just the number and size of the competitors does not always provide clear guidance to the correct competitive situation.

1. Consider the following hypothetical situations, identify the competitive situation represented, and then briefly explain what factors led you to this conclusion. The first one has been completed for you.

   a. Sam's Gas and Snacks is the only station located at the crossroads of a major highway and Interstate 17 going north and south. The closest town is located on the major highway five miles east. Their main target is travelers.

      Competitive Situation: *Monopolistic competition leaning toward geographic monopoly.*

      Explanation: *Even though Sam's Gas and Snacks probably attracts a large number of travelers, Sam's does not have a monopoly. There are other crossroads at which travelers could stop either before or after, if they properly plan. Travelers could also go five miles into town to make their purchases. Further, we know of no restrictions that would prevent competitors from locating across the road or right next door. Thus, we can conclude Sam's Gas and Snacks is competing in monopolistic competition.*

   b. Tender Care is a licensed day care center located in a city of 300,000 people. Tender Care has three centers operating in this city. There are about 15 similar day care centers operating in this city also. Some businesses have their own on-site day care centers for their employees. In addition, there are many individuals who conduct day care activities out of their own homes. Due to the number of day care operations, they all charge approximately the same price.

      Competitive Situation: ____

      Explanation: ____

____

____

____

____

Name ______________________________ Date ________________

Student Activity 8.2 (continued)

c. Fred Little has approximately 300 dairy cattle that he milks twice a day. Every morning at 9 a.m., the wholesaler stops on his route with his tanker truck and picks up Mr. Little's milk. The milk is then taken to the processing plant, where it is combined with hundreds of other dairy farmers' milk from around the area. Most of the milk is processed and put into bottles or cartons and shipped to local stores. Some of the milk is used to produce other dairy products.

Competitive Situation: ______________________________

Explanation: ______________________________

____

____

____

____

d. Clayton College has an enrollment of 1,000 students and is located in a small, midwestern town named Edina. Edina has a total population of 2,500 people. The nearest town is 20 miles away. Most of the residents shop locally, but they travel about once a month to the larger city and pick up the large-ticket items. Edina has one fairly good-size supply store named Miller's Market. The only other place in town where you might buy supplies is at the gas station/convenience store located on the edge of town. What competitive situation is Miller's Market experiencing?

Competitive Situation: ______________________________

Explanation: ______________________________

____

____

____

____

Name____________________________ Date__________________

Student Activity 8.2 (continued)

e. Iowa farmers can choose from five different manufacturers of farm implement equipment. Two of these manufacturers account for more than 80 percent of all the farm equipment sold in Iowa. These two manufacturers produce very similar equipment. Whenever one manufacturer has a sale, offers rebates, or offers special financing, the other manufacturer quickly follows with a similar program.

Competitive Situation: ____________________________

Explanation: ____________________________

2. Review the firms described in the situations above. What could each of them have done in order to get more control over their price strategy in order to make more profit?

a. ____________________________

b. ____________________________

c. ____________________________

d. ____________________________

e. ____________________________

Name ______________________________ Date ______________

Internet Activity #8

What is the purpose of the Federal Trade Commission, and where does it get its authority? Outline these legislative acts. Follow the path outlined below at the Internet address to find information about this topic. Use the space below for your answers.

www.ftc.gov

Antitrust/Competition
Profile of the Bureau of Competition

Section 9—Money

Introduction

What is money and what is it good for? Wow, anyone who asks this question must be pretty stupid, right? Well, that is true to a certain point. However, when we are studying economics, we are studying the decision-making behavior of individuals and their limited resources. As we discussed earlier, money is one of those limited resources. Money has many purposes, and that is what we will be looking at in this section.

Money as a Medium of Exchange

The most common use of money is as a **medium of exchange**, which is anything that members of a society are willing to accept in return for goods and services or as payment of a debt.

Money, by this definition, does not have to be paper, coins, or gold. There have been many things used as money throughout human history. Today, we use government paper and coins, along with checks, as payment. But, in earlier times, people used rocks, shells, animals, or anything else that was deemed scarce or valuable.

It would be impossible for a modern economy to function effectively without some type of medium of exchange. There are simply too many transactions that take place on a daily basis in the United States for bartering to work. **Bartering** is exchanging goods and services for other goods and services (example: trading a haircut for fixing a flat tire). Although some bartering does take place, it is a very, very small part of our economy. When people barter, much time and other resources are required before anyone can exchange one good or service for another.

Question: What are some bartering transactions that you are familiar with?

Money as a Unit of Account

When a country adopts a currency as a medium of exchange, it follows that it will also use it as the country's **unit of account**, that is, how an economy's prices are stated. For example, a dozen eggs might be priced at $0.85 or a pair of pants at $24.95.

Money as a Store of Value

When people or firms exchange their goods or services for money, they have something they can easily save for future needs. Whether they put their money in piggy banks, under their mattresses, or in banks, they can store the value of the previous trade until the time they need to purchase something.

The Money Cycle

When the U. S. Mint prints new dollars and stamps out new coins, it is not creating additional money, but rather it is replacing the bills and coins that wear out from changing hands so often. The cost of keeping currency in good shape is approximately $120 million a year.

Today, new coins are made at one of three U. S. Mint branches. Each Mint branch has its own mint mark that appears on each coin: **D** represents the Denver Mint, **S** represents the San Francisco Mint, and **P** (or no mark at all) represents the Philadelphia Mint.

The number and types of bills and coins demanded changes with the lifestyles and needs of consumers. In the 1960s, for example, vending machines became very popular, and more and more products were being sold through vending machines. Because of the increased use of vending machines, the demand for nickels, dimes, and quarters grew dramatically. Today, most vending machines take dollar bills and give change, so the demand for coins has dropped considerably. However, the popular use of Automated Teller Machines (ATMs) today has increased the demand for $10 and $20 bills.

THE MONEY CYCLE

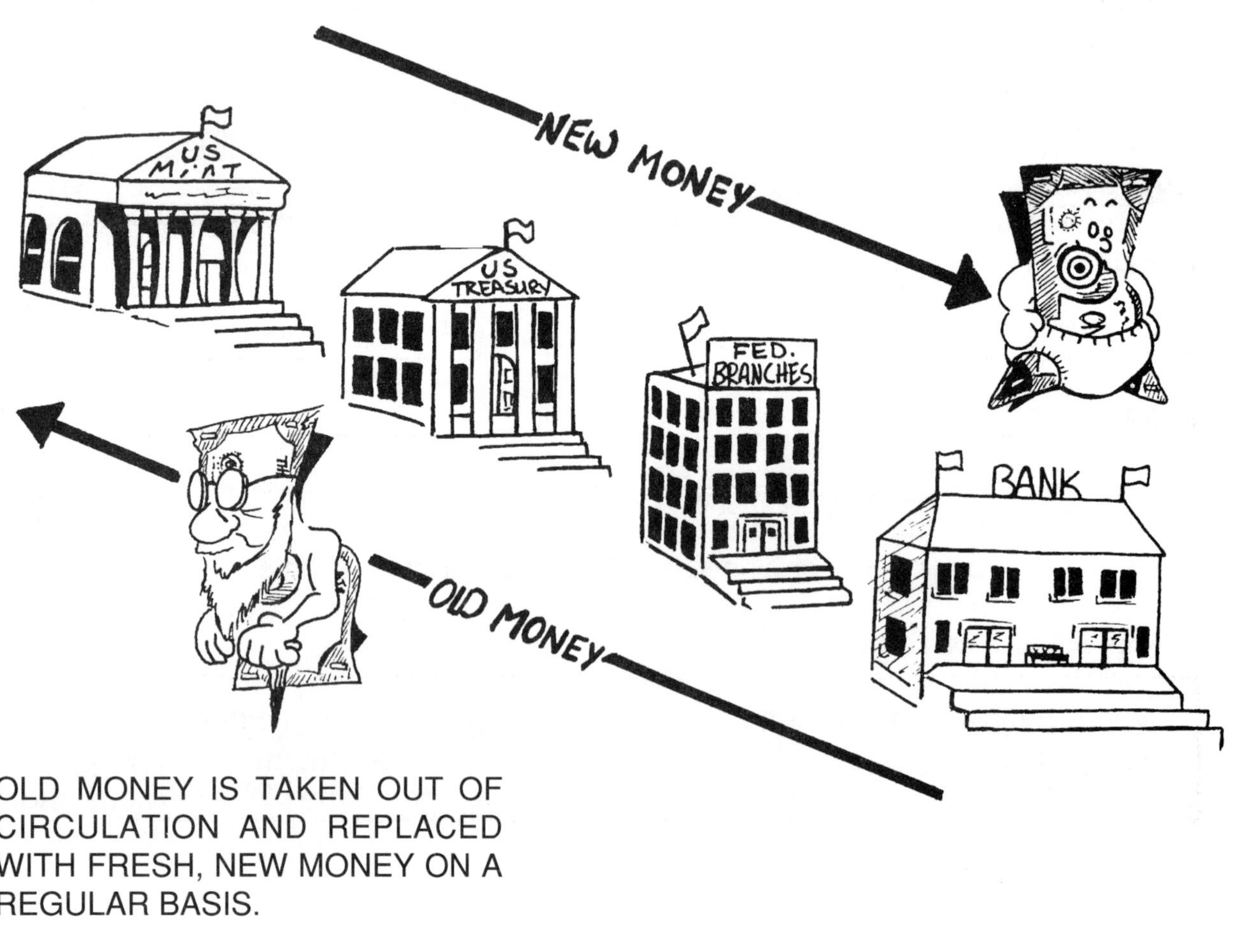

OLD MONEY IS TAKEN OUT OF CIRCULATION AND REPLACED WITH FRESH, NEW MONEY ON A REGULAR BASIS.

Name ______________________________ Date ____________________

Student Activity 9.1

1. Grab a handful of coins and identify at which branch of the U.S. Mint the coins were produced. (Don't worry if you can't find all of these types of coins.)

	Pennies	**Nickels**	**Dimes**	**Quarters**	**Half-Dollars**
a.	________	________	________	________	________
b.	________	________	________	________	________
c.	________	________	________	________	________
d.	________	________	________	________	________
e.	________	________	________	________	________

2. Whose picture is on the following bills? (Hint: You can go to a library or bank or use the Internet address given in Internet Activity #9.)

a. $1	________________	g. $100	________________
b. $2	________________	h. $500	________________
c. $5	________________	i. $1,000	________________
d. $10	________________	j. $5,000	________________
e. $20	________________	k. $10,000	________________
f. $50	________________	l. $100,000	________________

"Real success is finding your lifework in the work that you love." —David McCullough

Name ______________________ Date ______________

Student Activity 9.2

1. Research the history of money. Then write a report on (1) the silliest, strangest, or most unusual item that was used as a country's medium of exchange, (2) why it did not last as the country's medium of exchange, (3) whether the United States will ever become a totally cashless society, and (4) if it will, how this will affect our units of account and storage of value. Use the space below for your notes.

2. If you live close to a U. S. Mint branch, see if you can take a field trip or get some brochures or other information from the Mint.

Name________________________________ Date____________________

Internet Activity #9

What have the Treasury Department and the Federal Reserve done to make the new currency bills ($100, $50, and $20) counterfeit-proof? Follow the path outlined below at the Internet address to find information about this topic. Use the space below for your answers.

www.ustreas.gov

What's New

Section 10—Global Trade

Introduction

Our economy does not take place in a vacuum. It is important to realize this. Our trade policies affect employment and unemployment, monetary policies, government spending, budget-making, and peace-keeping policies.

Why Countries Trade With Each Other

There are many benefits that citizens enjoy because of trading with other countries. Americans drink coffee from Brazil and tea from China, and many Americans wear Swiss-made watches and watch Japanese-made televisions. Many Americans drive cars made in Japan and Germany. Furthermore, these cars and others made in America are powered by gasoline from Arab countries.

The people of the United States are very fortunate that we have almost all of the resources we need to produce everything we desire. Other countries may not be as lucky. Some countries cannot grow certain crops because of the weather, or they cannot produce everything because they simply do not have enough people to do so. It should be easy to understand why some countries need and want to trade, but why would the United States want to trade? The answer lays in the economic concepts of "The Principle of Absolute Advantage" and "The Law of Comparative Advantage."

The Principle of Absolute Advantage

The concept of **ABSOLUTE ADVANTAGE** comes from the fact that some individuals (or countries) can produce more of a good from given resources than can others.

For example, a Kansas farmer can grow more corn per acre than a farmer in Colombia, South America. However, the Colombian farmer can grow more coffee beans per acre than the Kansas farmer can grow. In this example, the Kansas farmer has an absolute advantage in corn production, and the Colombian farmer has an absolute advantage in coffee bean production.

In the above example, if Kansas farmers specialized in corn production, Colombian farmers specialized in coffee bean production, and the two countries traded their excess production with one another, then the citizens of both countries would be better off. The theory of specializing in what we can do fastest and cheapest is called absolute advantage.

The Law of Comparative Advantage

It is relatively easy to see that countries that have an absolute advantage in the production of a certain product can benefit from trading with one another, but what if one country has the absolute advantage in the production of all goods? Does it still make sense to trade with a country that does not have an absolute advantage in anything? The answer is probably yes, and this is explained by the **LAW OF COMPARATIVE ADVANTAGE**.

For example, suppose there is a highly-paid executive who is also very good at word processing. Suppose this executive were to hire a secretary to do the word processing for him, only to find out later that the secretary was only half as fast at word processing as the executive. Was it a good idea to hire a secretary who was less efficient in word processing than the boss? The executive can obviously make more money by devoting his time to managing and decision-making than he can doing word processing. Consequently, even though the executive has an absolute advantage in both managing and word processing, he has a larger **comparative advantage** with respect to managing.

Likewise, in global trade, one nation might have an absolute advantage in the production of two commodities but choose to import the item in which it has the lesser absolute advantage (or comparative advantage) and to export the item in which it has the greater absolute advantage.

"No nation was ever ruined by trade." —Benjamin Franklin

ABSOLUTE & COMPARATIVE ADVANTAGE

Name ______________________ Date ______________

Student Activity 10.1

Law of Comparative Advantage

List and explain two household chores your parents make you do that relate to the Law of Comparative Advantage.

1. Your household chore: ______________________

   Explanation: ______________________

____

____

____

____

2. Your household chore: ______________________

   Explanation: ______________________

____

____

____

____

3. Do you have an absolute or comparative advantage in doing something over someone else? Explain.

____

____

____

____

____

____

Name ______________________________ Date ______________

Student Activity 10.2

Go to your local hardware or building supply store. Look for products that were imported from other countries. Compare the prices to similar U.S.-produced products. If the prices differ greatly, explain why. If the prices are close, explain why.

Product	Foreign-Made Price	U.S.-Made Price
1. ____________________	__________	__________

Explanation: ____

____

Product	Foreign-Made Price	U.S.-Made Price
2. ____________________	__________	__________

Explanation: ____

____

Product	Foreign-Made Price	U.S.-Made Price
3. ____________________	__________	__________

Explanation: ____

____

Product	Foreign-Made Price	U.S.-Made Price
4. ____________________	__________	__________

Explanation: ____

____

Product	Foreign-Made Price	U.S.-Made Price
5. ____________________	__________	__________

Explanation: ____

____

Name__________________________________ Date____________________

Internet Activity #10

Identify who the United States' top five trading partners are and how much we import and export to them. Follow the path outlined below at the Internet address to find information about this topic.

www.doc.gov

DOC Bureaus
International Trade Administration
Trade Statistics
U.S. Foreign Trade Highlight
U.S. Aggregate Foreign Trade Data
Table 9 Top 50 Partners

Trade Partner	Imports	Exports
1. ____________	____________	____________
2. ____________	____________	____________
3. ____________	____________	____________
4. ____________	____________	____________
5. ____________	____________	____________

Section 11—The Economic Cycle

Introduction

Inflation and recession are recurring phases of a continuous economic cycle. Government economists work hard to predict the timing of these phases and also to help control their effects.

INFLATION occurs when prices rise because there is too much money in circulation and not enough goods and services to spend it on.

RECESSION occurs when prices go so high that people either cannot or will not pay the high prices. Demand goes down, and the economy declines as well.

DEPRESSION occurs when a recession fails to recover after an extended period of time.

The Economic Cycle

Step 1: If the demand for products (like computers) went up, but there were not enough products available, then manufacturers and retailers would probably increase prices. This is because some people would pay more to get what they want.

Step 2: People (including the workers making computers) will soon demand higher wages so that they can afford the products they desire at the new higher prices. The cost of producing products rises because of increased wages, and producers pass the increased production costs on to the customers in the form of increased selling prices.

Step 3: When the selling prices of computers and other products rise so high that people either are not willing or cannot pay, then they stop buying. As fewer products are needed, manufacturers start to lay off workers.

Step 4: Unemployed people buy less of everything, and the economy continues to slow down. This is known as a recession. But now computer dealers and others get desperate to sell their inventory, so they reduce the prices and offer special sales.

Step 5: As prices decrease, more people are wanting to buy, especially since they have done without for a period of time. Consequently, demand increases sharply, manufacturers and retailers increase their selling prices, workers demand more money, and the cycle repeats itself once again.

Controlling the Economic Cycle

Most countries today do not let their economic cycles run unchecked, because it could lead to a major worldwide depression like the one that followed the 1929 stock market crash in the United States.

Instead, governments and central banks change their monetary policies to affect what is happening in the economy. In the United States, the government body charged with the responsibility of controlling monetary policy is the **Federal Reserve** (often referred to as "the Fed"). The Fed's most effective tool for dealing with inflation and recession is its power to adjust the interest rates at which banks can borrow money. This then affects the rates at which businesses and consumers can borrow money.

Inflation is often fueled by political pressures. A growing economy creates jobs and reduces unemployment. Politicians are almost always in favor of reducing unemployment for their voters. Consequently, politicians urge the Federal Reserve to adopt an easy monetary policy that stimulates the economy—in other words, the Fed is urged to reduce interest rates.

Once inflation really starts to take off, the most effective method for ending the inflation is for the Fed to induce an economic downturn or a recession. The Federal Reserve does this by reducing the money supply via increasing interest rates.

To keep inflation from getting out of control or keep recession from cutting too deeply, the Federal Reserve makes small, periodic adjustments in interest rates.

INFLATION
WE BETTER GET ONE NOW BEFORE THE PRICES GO HIGHER
WEANIE BABIES
3.00
4.00
10.00
20.00
TOO MUCH DEMAND, TOO LITTLE SUPPLY

Who Wins and Who Loses During Inflationary Times?

During periods of inflation, big debtors make out well. Many times the money they pay back is only worth half as much as it was worth when they borrowed it. Inflation also prompts investors to buy things they can resell at huge profits, like artwork and real estate, rather than putting their money into companies that can create new products and jobs.

The people who are hit the hardest during periods of inflation are those living on fixed incomes. These are often retired people whose retirement incomes are determined by salaries or wages earned in less inflationary times. Their standards of living can be swiftly eroded by high inflation, sometimes even forcing them to sell their homes or to take other drastic economic measures.

Name______________________________ Date____________________

Student Activity 11.1

The "Rule of 72" is a reliable guide to the impact of inflation. It is based on dividing 72 by the annual inflation rate to find out the number of years it will take the price of something to double. For example, if you bought an antique chair for $100, and the annual inflation rate is 5 percent, how long would it take for the chair to be worth $200? Using the Rule of 72, divide 72 by 5 and get 14.4. It would take about 14 years for the chair's worth to double.

At the different inflation rates given below, calculate the number of years it will take to double the product purchase price.

1. If you bought a house for $150,000 and the annual inflation rate was 4 percent, how long would it take before the house, under good maintenance, would be worth $300,000?

   ____

2. If you bought a Picasso painting at last week's auction for $200,000 and the annual inflation rate is 10 percent, how long would it take to double your money?

   ____

3. If you went to the car show and bought a 1965 Mustang in mint condition for $25,000 and the annual inflation rate was 8 percent, when would your investment double?

   ____

4. If your grandmother gave you her wedding ring, it was appraised at $1,200, and the annual inflation rate was 6 percent, how many years would it be before it was worth $2,400?

   ____

5. If you bought an antique lamp for $3,000 and the inflation rate was 3 percent, how many years would it be before your investment doubled in value?

   ____

Name________________________ Date________________

Student Activity 11.2

The Effects of Inflation

1. If Mrs. Poorman were living on a fixed pension of $500 per month, how would she fare if the inflation rate increased?

____

____

____

2. Why did homeowners who bought their houses before 1980 benefit from inflation?

____

____

____

3. If we were to experience a 10 percent-per-year inflation rate for the next 10 years, what effect would that have on the purchasing power of the dollar at the end of that time?

____

____

____

4. If you had a nest egg of $100,000 and all signs pointed to a period of prolonged inflation, what should you do with your money?

____

____

____

Name ______________________________ Date ____________________

Internet Activity #11

Inflation is a period of generally rising prices. The Consumer Price Index is a way of measuring inflation. The government calculates the value of the same "basket of goods" monthly. What is the recent CPI trend in Dallas-Ft. Worth, and what does this represent? Research and write a short report on the history of the CPI. Follow the path outlined below at the Internet address to find information about this topic. Use the space below for your notes.

http://stats.bls.gov/blshome.html

Data
Most Requested Services
Region VI–Dallas
Dallas-Ft. Worth, all items
Retrieve

Section 12—Government Production of Goods and Services

Introduction

In our market-directed economy, producers provide goods and services that consumers demand as long as they can collect the selling price and can make a profit. However, there are some products and services that are desired by consumers but that are not profitable for producers to offer. With other products and services, it is not easy or possible to collect the selling price. When either of these factors exist, sometimes the government will provide the product or service or subsidize a company to provide the product or service. The government might also provide goods or services that are not feasible for individual consumers to own.

Public Goods

Goods and services produced by the government are referred to as **public goods**. One reason for public goods is that it is not feasible or efficient to recover the full costs by charging the people who use the products or services directly. Roads and highways would be a good example of this situation. Another reason for public goods is that the goods or services cannot be sold for a high enough price to cover production and distribution costs, but they are of sufficient importance to society. Libraries and public schools would be a good example of this situation. Our founding fathers realized that some products and services must clearly be public goods. National defense is an obvious example. It is just not feasible for individuals to purchase Patriot missiles to protect their homes against attacks from foreign enemies.

Other Benefactors

Goods and services sometimes benefit people other than the purchasers. The Internet and e-mail not only benefit the subscriber but also provide benefits to everyone who e-mails that person. The subscriber pays for the monthly connection, but all e-mailers receive benefits from their connections, even though they do not pay for them. Of course, most of them have Internet and e-mail connections of their own, which they do pay for, but the more people who have Internet and e-mail, the more use one's own connection is.

Consequently, the Internet and e-mail provide benefits not only to the purchaser but to other people as well.

If goods and services are supplied by private enterprises, the price must cover their costs. Buyers must pay for the total costs of production and distribution. If people are unwilling to pay the price, the goods and services are not produced. However, there are some products for which the benefits are so significant that their production is justified, even if buyers are unwilling to pay the price.

If our country did not have a literate population, it could not operate industries efficiently or provide the professional services needed by people. This is the justification for the government to pay for education. Because of the benefits resulting from education, families are not required to pay the full costs of their children's schooling. The government pays most of the costs for public education from the collection of taxes from everyone. Public health services, medical research, and postal services are other examples where services benefit people other than those directly receiving the services.

Public Goods and Equality

Sometimes public goods are provided in order to meet the goal of greater equality. Public transportation, for example, is most heavily used by lower-income groups, including young people and the elderly. This is one of the justifications for government subsidies to public transit systems. It helps to achieve the socio-economic goal of greater economic equality.

An alternate way to achieve the goal of greater equality would be to give direct subsidies to low-income people. In some ways, this might satisfy the goal of equality more efficiently. Income supplements might help low-income people more than subsidized bus fares because such supplements permit them to choose the best transportation means for their particular needs.

The argument over which is the best approach—income supplements or public services—will go on forever. On the surface, income supplements and choices seem to be the fairest ways of achieving economic equality, but there may be many other costs involved. For example, if a low-income person decided he or she would like an automobile of his or her own for maximum flexibility, he or she would also incur other expenses, such as gas, insurance, and maintenance costs, just to name a few. In order for supplements to be large enough to cover all the associated costs, the tax burden on the rest of society would have to increase.

> "When government accepts responsibility for people, then people no longer take responsibility for themselves." —George Pataki

Name______________________________ Date____________________

Student Activity 12.1

1. List five public goods you have utilized in the past month. Put a "yes" or "no" next to each, indicating if this public good could have been obtained through the private sector.

   a. ____

   b. ____

   c. ____

   e. ____

   f. ____

2. Why does the government subsidize public transportation when most people do not use it?

3. What are some goods or services that you have benefitted from but that you or your family have not used or paid for?

4. What are some goods or services provided or subsidized by the government that help foster greater equality among the citizens of the United States?

Name ______________________________ Date ________________

Student Activity 12.2

Have a representative from your local public bus company come and speak to your class. Try to find out the following information.

1. How is the bus company funded?

____

____

2. What percentage of income comes from fares?

____

3. What percentage of income comes from subsidies?

____

4. Where do the subsidies come from: local, state, or federal government?

____

Additional notes:

____

____

____

____

____

____

____

____

____

____

____

____

____

Name______________________________ Date____________________

Internet Activity #12

For which industries could a business obtain reports pertinent to determining market potential? Follow the path outlined below at the Internet address to find information about this topic. Describe five specific reports that would be useful to businesses when determining market potential.

http://www.findsvp.com

Market Looks
Your Choice
find/SPV Marketlook
view free summary

Name______________________________ Date____________________

Basic Economics Review

Place the correct term from the word bank on the line next to the corresponding definition.

WORD BANK

Absolute Advantage	Inelastic Demand	Planned System
Allocate	Inflation	Profit
Bartering	Interest	Public Goods
Capital	Labor	Pure
Corporation	Land	Recession
Cyclical	Law of Comparative Advantage	Rents
Demand Curve	Law of Diminishing Demand	Resources
Depression	Macroeconomics	Rule of 72
Discouraged Workers	Market Equilibrium Point	Scarcity
Dishonest Nonworkers	Market System	Seasonal
Economics	Medium of Exchange	Sole Proprietorship
Elastic Demand	Microeconomics	Structural
Entrepreneurship	Mint	Substitutes
Federal Reserve	Monopolistic	Supply Curve
Frictional	Monopoly	Unit of Account
Geographic Monopoly	Oligopoly	Wants
Induced	Partnership	

1. Individual decision-making about the allocation of resources ________________
2. The U.S. government body charged with controlling monetary policy ________________
3. To divide among or to distribute in shares ________________
4. The means to accomplish something ________________
5. Societal decision-making about the allocation of resources ________________
6. The study of the ways that individuals and societies allocate their limited resources in order to better satisfy their unlimited wants ________________
7. We can never have all we want of every good and service. ________________
8. The mental and physical efforts applied to the production of goods and services ________________
9. When prices rise because there is too much money in circulation and not enough goods and services to spend it on ________________
10. Unemployment that is caused by government policy ________________
11. All relatively permanent improvements made to land ________________

Name ______________________________ Date ____________________

12. Individuals who would like to go back to work, but who have given up looking for a new job ____________________ ____________________
13. Exchanging goods and services for other goods and services ____________________
14. Payment for risk-taking or entrepreneurship ____________________
15. What and how much to produce and the worth of goods and services is decided by private buyers and sellers. ____________________
16. Government planners decide what and how much to produce and how it will be distributed. ____________________
17. A business owned by one person ____________________
18. Unemployment that happens naturally ____________________
19. An organization sanctioned by state laws and considered a legal entity separate and distinct from the owners ____________________
20. The environmental resource ____________________
21. Shows the amount of goods or services consumers are willing to purchase at various prices ____________________
22. When prices go so high that people either cannot or will not pay, demand goes down, and the economy declines. ____________________
23. One of three locations where U.S. coins are stamped out ____________________
24. As the price fluctuates up or down, demand remains constant. ____________________
25. Shows the amount of goods or services producers are willing to make available and sell at various prices ____________________
26. Market situation in which there is only one seller, and there are no substitutes for the product ____________________
27. Payment for capital ____________________
28. Individuals who say they are looking for work in order to get unemployment compensation but who have no real intention of taking a new job ____________________ ____________________
29. Two or more individuals combining to form a business ____________________
30. Things that are needed or desired ____________________
31. Unemployment that occurs because some products or businesses are in demand during only part of the year ____________________
32. Alternative goods or services ____________________
33. Payments for the use of land ____________________
34. Type of competition in which there are many buyers and sellers, the products are very similar or identical, and entry into the market is relatively easy ____________________

Name ______________________ Date ______________

35. As demand price goes up, so will the supply of a given good or service; as demand price goes down, so will supply. ______________
36. Type of competition in which there are few sellers who offer very similar products ______________
37. The point at which the quantity and the price that sellers are willing to offer is equal to the quantity and price that buyers are willing to accept ______________
38. When there is only one provider within a certain geographic area ______________
39. Anything that members of a society are willing to accept in return for goods and services or as payment of a debt ______________
40. The risk-taking resource ______________
41. How an economy's prices are stated ______________
42. As the price fluctuates, so does demand; as prices increase, demand decreases, and as prices go down, demand goes up. ______________
43. The fact that some individuals or countries can produce more of a good from given resources than others can ______________
44. The fact that a person or country will trade with another person or country for certain items because they have less absolute advantage in producing those items than other items ______________
45. Type of competition in which sellers offer different products and sellers believe they have competition ______________
46. Unemployment that is the result of the cycle of good and poor economic times ______________
47. When a recession fails to recover after an extended period of time ______________
48. Unemployment that occurs when the skills of the potential employee no longer match the needs of potential employers ______________
49. Goods and services produced by the government ______________
50. A method for determining how long it will take the price of something to double ______________

Answer Key to Student Activities

Student Activity 1.1 (page 3)

1. Micro
2. Macro
3. Micro
4. Micro
5. Macro
6. Macro
7. Macro
8. Micro
9. Micro
10. Macro
11. Micro
12. Macro
13. Micro
14. Micro
15. Micro

Student Activity 1.2 (page 4)

Answers will vary. Possible answers include:

1. Go to school, what to wear, what television shows to watch
2. Budgeting and spending, how to deal with hostile countries, regulation of products like cigarettes
3. Time, money, energy, or skills
4. Make a schedule to set aside time, do chores to earn an allowance, have a job, take lessons to develop skills, or practice skills
5. Games, candy, clothes, or money

Activity 2.1 (page 8)

1. \$18, \$300, \$318
2. \$400
3. \$420, \$441, \$463.05, \$486.20, \$510.51
4. 150 interest (30 x 5)
   650 total (500 + 150)
   \$10.83 per month (650 ÷ 60)

Student Activity 2.2 (page 9)

Answers will vary, but may include the following:

1. Labor:
   a. teacher
   b. staff
   c. maintenance
2. Land:
   a. property
   b. water
   c. landscaping
3. Capital:
   a. buildings
   b. parking lot
   c. equipment
4. Entrepreneurship:
   a. school board
   b. teachers' time
   c. support staff effort

Activity 3.1 (page 13)

Answers will vary. Examples include:

1. Brute force—An older brother takes the last piece of cake.
2. Queuing—You wait in the lunch line, hoping they do not run out of your favorite food.
3. Random selection—The teacher picks three student names out of a hat to go on a special field trip.

4. Tradition—The student with the best grades in class has always been given the opportunity to work in the school library.
5. Equal shares—Dad divides up the family pizza.
6. Need—All that the class has earned for the class picnic is given to a family whose house burned down along with all their possessions.

Activity 4.1 (pages 18–19)

1. The sole proprietor would receive $100,000.
2. You—$50,000 (1/2), Alice—$30,000 (3/5), Mark—$20,000 (2/5)
3. You—$40,000 (1/2), Alice—$24,000 (3/5), Mark—$16,000 (2/5)
4.

$8,000	$8,000	$8,000
$12,000	$27,000	$52,000
$8	$8	$8
$3	$6.75	$13

Activity 4.2 (page 20)

Plan	**$30,000 Income**		**$15,000 Income**	
	Mary	**Carla**	**Mary**	**Carla**
Equal Division	$15,000	$15,000	$7,500	$7,500
Original Investment	$18,000	$12,000	$9,000	$6,000
Time Devoted	$20,000	$10,000	$10,000	$5,000

Activity 5.1 (page 23)

Answers will vary. Possible answers include:

1. Highways
2. Public schools
3. Public television and radio
4. Welfare programs
5. National defense
6. Government salaries
7. Subsidies to other countries in need
8. National parks
9. Space program
10. Medical research

Activity 5.2 (page 24)

Answers will vary, but may include the following:

1. Public schools—education
2. Highways—good roads
3. National parks—vacation spots
4. Unemployment insurance—security
5. Social Security—retirement funds
6. Police and Fire departments—security
7. Auto regulation—safety
8. Military—security
9. National Endowment for the Arts—culture
10. Medical research—health

Activity 6.1 (page 31)

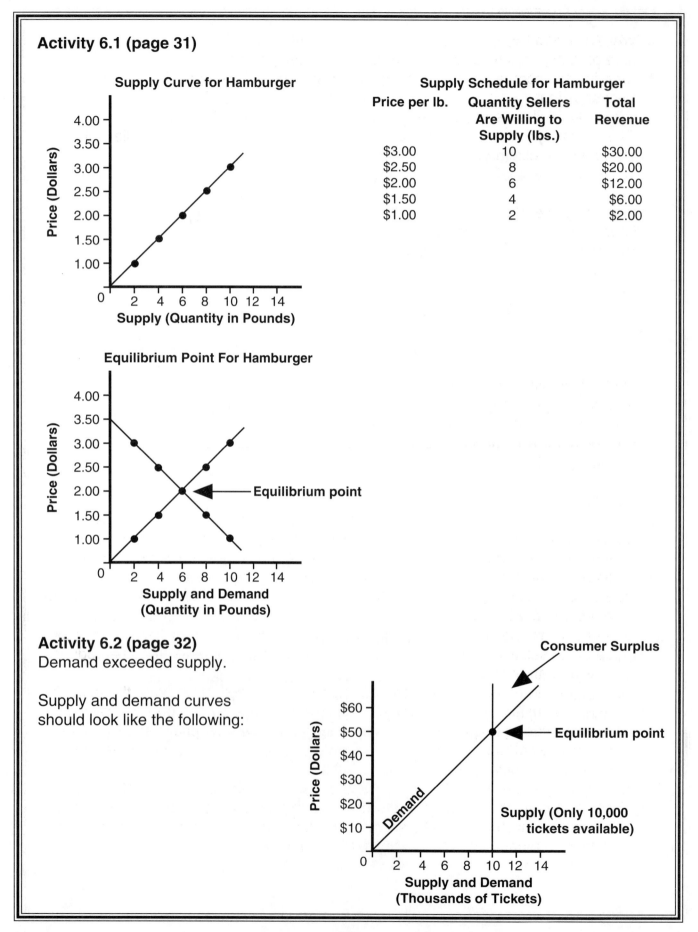

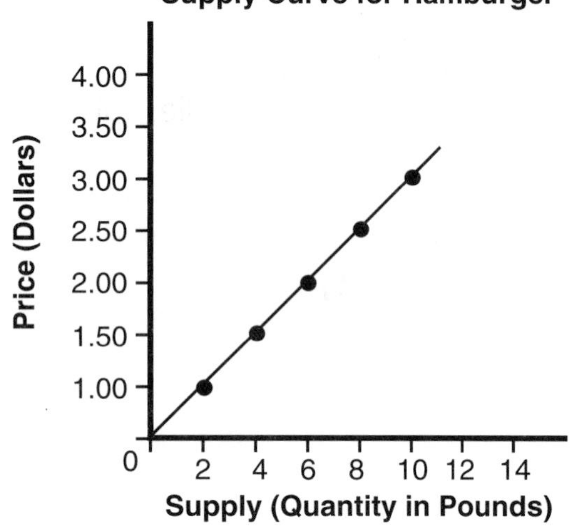

Supply Schedule for Hamburger

Price per lb.	Quantity Sellers Are Willing to Supply (lbs.)	Total Revenue
$3.00	10	$30.00
$2.50	8	$20.00
$2.00	6	$12.00
$1.50	4	$6.00
$1.00	2	$2.00

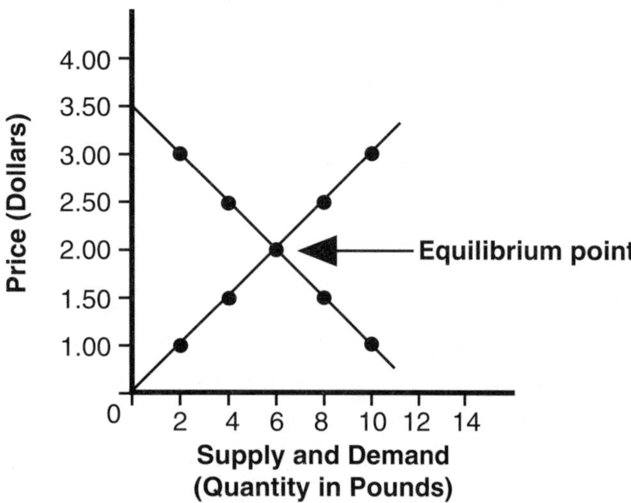

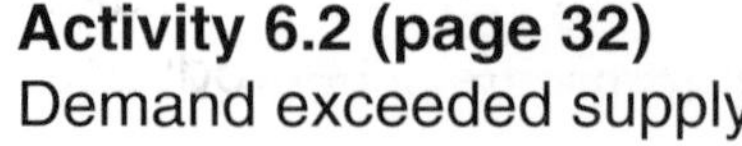

Activity 6.2 (page 32)

Demand exceeded supply.

Supply and demand curves should look like the following:

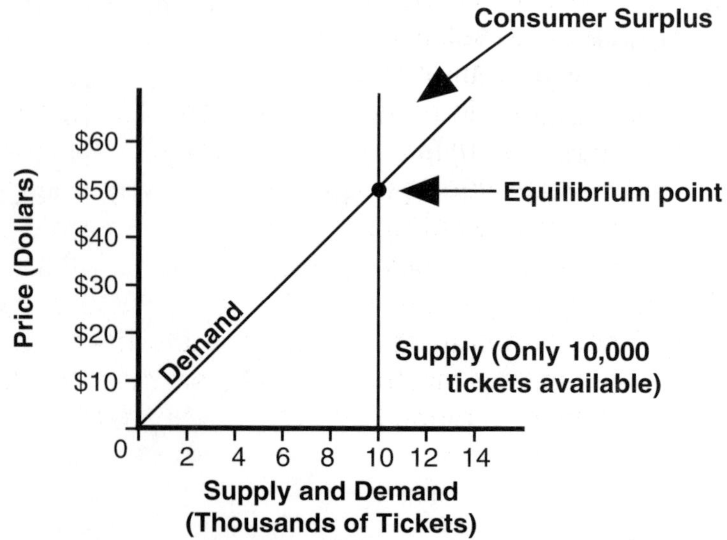

Activity 7.1 (page 36)

1. Loss of family income and possible damage to self-esteem
2. Loss in tax income, because of less wages, and an increase in unemployment compensation
3. The worker will have more time and willingness to find a better job.
4. Trim down work force, which they may have been hesitant to do earlier; also an opportunity to eliminate those less productive workers
5. No. He is not available for work.

Activity 7.2 (page 37)

1. Structural
2. Frictional
3. Cyclical
4. Seasonal
5. Structural
6. Induced

Activity 8.1 (page 42)

1. Answers will vary. Possible answers include:
   A. corn, wheat, pork bellies; breakfast cereal; gasoline; hotel with no others for 80 miles
   B. many; few or many; few; none
   C. identical; different in eyes of customers; very similar; unique
   D. weak; strong; powerful; very powerful
   E. none; some; some w/ care; complete
   F. easy; somewhat difficult money; difficult money; impossible
   G. either; tends to be elastic; tends to be inelastic; either

Activity 8.2 (pages 43–45)

1. a. Given
   b. Monopolistic competition—There are many competitors offering day care. Being licensed, they should all offer similar services. Any one day care center might adjust its prices higher due to location, facilities, or quality of service.
   c. Pure competition—There are many small producers of milk. No single producer can affect the market, either through price changes or pulling out of the market. The same holds true if another small producer would enter the market. It would not make sense to sell at a lower price since the individual could sell all he or she produces now at market price.
   d. Geographic monopoly—As long as residents are unwilling to drive the extra 20 miles (40 miles per round trip), Miller's Market enjoys a monopoly situation. The major advantage for Miller's is that they can charge higher prices as long as their profits are not too high, which would invite competition or encourage residents to change their buying habits.
   e. Oligopoly—There are two manufacturers who dominate the market. They are selling somewhat similar products that perform similar tasks. Typical in an oligopoly situation is that the major players follow the leader in pricing strategy; no firm wants to lose its market share that it has taken so long to build up.

2. This answer is alluded to in the above answers, but the main key to getting more control over price is to better satisfy your target market. A firm in any competitive situation needs to establish and maintain a meaningful competitive advantage; it is done through continuous product improvement. The most difficult competitive situation in which to get a meaningful competitive advantage is pure competition.

Activity 9.1 (page 49)

1. Answers will vary.
2. a. George Washington
   b. Thomas Jefferson
   c. Abraham Lincoln
   d. Alexander Hamilton
   e. Andrew Jackson
   f. Ulysses S. Grant
   g. Benjamin Franklin
   h. William McKinley
   i. Grover Cleveland
   j. James Madison
   k. Salman P. Chase
   l. Woodrow Wilson

Activity 9.2 (page 50)

1. Teacher check report.

Acitivity 10.1 (page 54)

Answers will vary.

Activity 10.2 (page 55)

Answers will vary, but explanations should be based on absolute and comparative advantages.

Activity 11.1 (page 59)

1. 18 years 2. 7 years 3. 9 years 4. 12 years 5. 24 years

Activity 11.2 (page 60)

1. She would not fare well. Her costs are increasing, but her income is not.
2. Interest rates were low, and inflation caused house values to increase.
3. You could purchase more for your dollar now.
4. Invest in fixed assets, such as antiques, a house, etc.

Activity 12.1 (page 64)

Answers will vary.

Activity 12.2 (page 65)

Answers will vary.

Basic Economics Review (pages 67–69)

1. Microeconomics
2. Federal Reserve
3. Allocate
4. Resources
5. Macroeconomics
6. Economics
7. Scarcity
8. Labor
9. Inflation
10. Induced
11. Capital
12. Discouraged Workers
13. Bartering
14. Profit
15. Market System
16. Planned System
17. Sole Proprietorship
18. Frictional
19. Corporation
20. Land
21. Demand Curve
22. Recession
23. Mint
24. Inelastic Demand
25. Supply Curve
26. Monopoly
27. Interest
28. Dishonest Nonworkers
29. Partnership
30. Wants
31. Seasonal
32. Substitutes
33. Rents
34. Pure
35. Law of Diminishing Demand
36. Oligopoly
37. Market Equilibrium Point
38. Geographic Monopoly
39. Medium of Exchange
40. Entrepreneurship
41. Unit of Account
42. Elastic Demand
43. Absolute Advantage
44. Law of Comparative Advantage
45. Monopolistic
46. Cyclical
47. Depression
48. Structural
49. Public Goods
50. Rule of 72

Answer Key to Internet Activities

To the Teacher:

You should access the Internet addresses before making the assignments. By doing this, you will be sure the sites are still active and will be able to better answer students' questions. The sites frequently change in information and style. The students should also be encouraged to search and find additional sites for information (extra credit might be given for this).

#1 (page 5)

Answers will vary, depending on which reports the students read. The information is updated weekly. Students should research trends such as prices, interest rates, consumer spending, etc. This is the first Internet Activity, so the students should be allowed to explore. Even though we have not gotten in-depth yet, this activity will give the students exposure to upcoming concepts. Spotting trends is an important part of using economic information.

#2 (page 10)

This is an exciting Internet site for most students because it is the CIA. Students should research and report on economic growth, wages, prices, unemployment, and their influence on purchase decisions.

#3 (page 15)

For those students who are not familiar with the workings of the Internet, this is a great site to visit. The history and evolution of the Internet should be discussed. Then the pricing and non-pricing, along with payment mechanisms, should be addressed.

#4 (page 21)
For a restaurant chain, the important monthly economic indicators would include retail trade, consumer price index, and unemployment. Students should report on why they selected the indicators they did, along with why they think these are important.

#5 (page 25)
This Internet site lets the students think about and explore career opportunities. Income is not the only measurement of success or guide to the best possible career, as we teachers know. The students should be encouraged to look at as many careers as possible.

#6 (page 33)
The student should check out at least six to eight hotels in San Francisco, along with the amenities that come with each. Then a comparison of prices and features should be done to figure out what would be the best value. The students should address the concept of substitutes and their impact on price.

#7 (page 38)
Answers will vary, depending on which articles students access. The key words would be "personal computers and price." Let the students know that not all the articles they find are going to be relevant to this assignment.

#8 (page 46)
It is supposed to prevent practices that restrain competition. Its authority comes from the FTC Act and the Clayton Act.

#9 (page 51)
There are security threads, a water mark that appears when the bill is held up to the light, a larger portrait, and color-changing ink, among other anti-counterfeit measures.

#10 (page 56)
Answers as of October 1998.
a. Canada
b. Japan
c. Mexico
d. China
e. United Kingdom

#11 (page 61)
Answers will vary according to what the economy is at the time.
1. As of July 1998—CPI 154.2
2. The trend is upward.

#12 (page 66)
1. Reports are available on most industries.
2. The five reports the students choose will vary.